AF428240

Trade and Commerce in Ancient China

The Grand Canal and The Silk Road

Ancient China Books for Kids

Children's Ancient History

Speedy Publishing LLC

40 E. Main St. #1156

Newark, DE 19711

www.speedypublishing.com

Copyright 2017

The great and complex Chinese civilization has traded with the rest of the world for thousands of years. How did the merchants travel, and what did they trade? Read on and learn more!

Ming Porcelain Vases

TRADE AND CHINA

China has always produced almost every-thing the nation needed, from food to clothing to pottery. But there were special goods that were not easy to grow or create in China, and precious things like jewels in other lands, so merchants set out to get them. They would take Chinese-made goods to far-off places and trade them for what they found there.

Chinese merchants carried silk, coral, pearls, jade, fine porcelain and tea to far-off lands. They traded mainly for gold and silver and for jewels and similar goods that were both valuable and easy to carry.

Chinese Merchants

No matter where traders went, there were robbers who would try to take away what they had. So merchants usually went in large groups along established routes on land or by sea, with soldiers to protect them, to keep safe.

THE SILK ROAD

The great land road from China to the Middle East and then to Europe was called The Silk Road. It followed what are now the northern borders of China, India, and then Persia, and its western end was in what is now Turkey.

Long caravans of horses and camels carried loads of goods on their backs in both directions. At regular intervals there were cities or other safe places where travellers could rest or get supplies.

Camels and people walking on the silk road

Chinese making silk cloth

The route was named for the cloth that Europeans valued highly and that could only be found in the Orient. At this time, Europeans did not know that silk is made from the threads of the cocoons of silkworms.

EXPANSION OF THE SILK ROAD

Routes from China to the Middle East had been in use for centuries, but the Silk Road became really important starting in the third century BCE. This was the time of a great expansion of the trade in silk.

old silk road

A LONG ROAD

The Silk Road was more than 4,000 miles long, and merchants and all the people with them had to walk or ride horses or camels for their whole journey. The caravan routes were not good enough for wagons or carts.

However, few merchants actually travelled from one end of the Silk Road to the other. Most merchants started from their home city and went to a city a few weeks' or months' travel along the Silk Road. There they would trade with other merchants and then head home with what those merchants had brought that far. Then those merchants would take the goods further.

Chinese Merchants

The Silk Road was not a single road, but many routes that let you choose how to go from this city to the next one. You could choose the slow, safer route, or the faster route that was more dangerous, because that's where the robbers were waiting.

Grand Canal China

THE GRAND CANAL

The Grand Canal is a waterway the Chinese built to carry trade between Beijing and Hangzhou, over a thousand miles to the south. The canal also connects China's two major rivers, the Yellow and the Yangtze.

The canal made it easy to ship grain from the farmlands of south China to the capital city in the north. This let the emperors feed their armies. And from the cities manufactured goods could travel south for the people who wanted them.

Grand Canal China

Yangzhou Modern Grand Canal

Parts of the Grand Canal are even older, but the whole canal was completed in 609 CE. Millions of laborers worked to build it, and many of them died while working on the canal. It was largely rebuilt in the 15th century. The Grand Canal is the longest waterway humans have ever built.

TRADING BY SEA

Trading with ships really changed once the Chinese invented the compass. This meant they could sail away until they were out of sight of land, and still have a good chance of finding their way back again.

Chinese Junk Keying

Some chinese travel in fishing boats

There were two main routes for trading by sea. One went south along the coast of Vietnam, and the other went east to the Philippine islands and then south to Indonesia. Ships using either route could pass through the Straits of Malacca to go further west, toward India.

The Spanish traders from Europe found a new route. They arrived in Chinese territory from the east, from Mexico, and their treasure ships sailed back east when they were full. In Mexico or Central America the cargo would be carried to the Atlantic coast and put on ships there that would carry the wealth of China home to Spain.

Each sailing trip from Europe to China, and back again, would take more than a year.

Traders from Europe

Admiral Zheng He

THE TREASURE FLEET

One of the most remarkable trading adventures happened in the 15th century. Admiral Zheng He led a fleet of enormous ships out from China on trading missions to India, Arabia, East Africa, and possibly further.

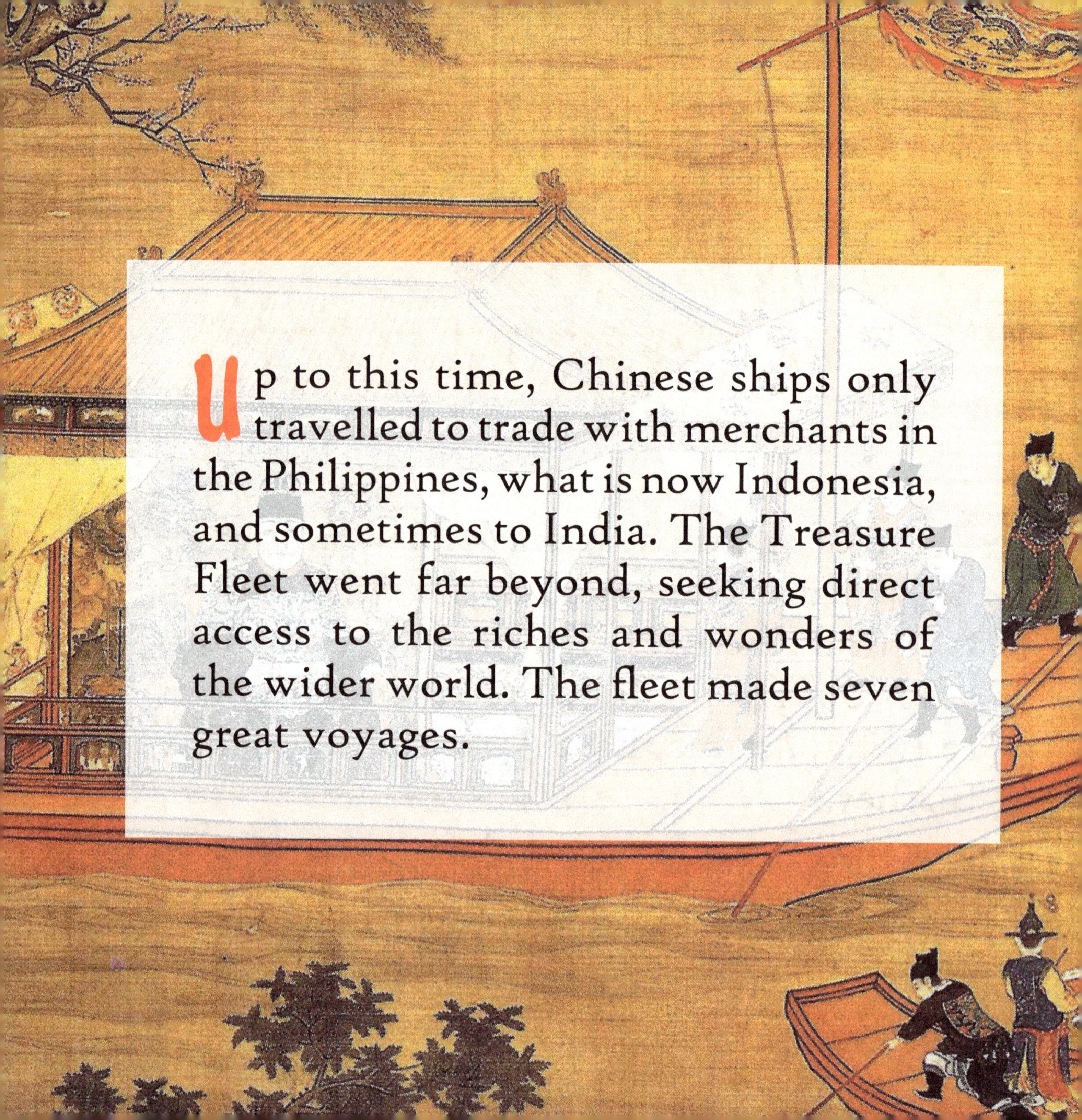

Up to this time, Chinese ships only travelled to trade with merchants in the Philippines, what is now Indonesia, and sometimes to India. The Treasure Fleet went far beyond, seeking direct access to the riches and wonders of the wider world. The fleet made seven great voyages.

Treasure Fleet

The ships of the Treasure Fleet were huge junks, much larger than any other ships of their time. They carried a large crew of both sailors and soldiers, and great amounts of cargo to trade. They could bring back riches and rarities, including even giraffes!

The Treasure Fleet made seven great voyages, and each trip took two or three years. The fleet traded with major centers like today's Calcutta, and also with villages and towns along the eastern coast of Africa. These visits greatly increased China's fame in the world.

The Chinese fleet had to navigate through waters for which they had no charts, and sometimes had to fight off fleets of pirate ships. Severe storms put the construction of the ships to the test.

During the seventh voyage, Admiral Zheng He died and was buried at sea. The emperor who had ordered the fleet to be built had already died, and the new emperor felt that the fleet was far too expensive to continue. China was facing great pressure from the Mongol empire to the north, and the emperor needed all his resources for that struggle.

But the emperor also had all the ships destroyed, as well as the dockyards where they had been built and repaired. He had all the official records of the voyages destroyed, as well. It was like he wanted to get rid of all evidence of this great adventure that the previous emperor had started.

ortunately for us, there are records in India and Africa, and some written records of the voyages that escaped destruction. Otherwise we would know little or nothing of the amazing Treasure Fleet.

TRADE WITH EUROPE

Many European countries established trading stations in or near China, bringing what they could from their own countries and bringing back tea, spices, porcelain, silk, and other valuable goods. The Dutch were the dominant force in European trade with China, but English, Spanish, Portuguese, and even Swedish traders were also very active.

Ethalion 1802

Sometimes the European traders fought against each other to gain control of the Chinese market. Sometimes a change in who was emperor meant a change in which European traders had the best luck.

Some European countries had their trading centers in what are now the cities of Hong Kong, Guangzhou, and Macao. Others had forts and trading posts in Taiwan or other islands nearby, or as far away as the islands of Indonesia.

CHINA FROM CHINA

Europeans highly valued porcelain and other fine Chinese goods. These first travelled toward Europe along the Silk Road, but once trade routes by sea were available, that's the way porcelain went. It was much heavier than silk or jewels, and so it was better to send it by ship.

Among the porcelain goods Europeans highly valued were:

Chinese porcelains

Batavia Ware

BATAVIA WARE

Batavia ware was very popular with the Dutch. It was a rich brown on the outside. Batavia, in what is now Indonesia, was the Dutch headquarters in Asia, so for people in the Netherlands, this material, although from China, seemed to come from Batavia.

Song and Yuan Porcelain

Beautiful porcelain from this period (around 900 to 1350 CE) were so much in demand that almost all of it was created for export. Relatively few examples of porcelain from this period are actually in China, and the greatest collection in the world is in the Topkapi Museum in Turkey.

Song and Yuan porcelain

MORE THAN TRADE

The contact merchants from China made with merchants from Europe involved more than physical goods. There was a great trade in ideas, ranging from scientific thoughts to inventions to philosophy and religion. The whole world would have been a much poorer place without the trade with China.

Read more Baby Professor books, like *How Did Your Chinese Ancestors Live?* and *The Chinese Festivals*, to learn more about life in China in this period.

Visit
BABY PROFESSOR
EDUCATION KIDS
www.BabyProfessorBooks.com
to download Free Baby Professor eBooks
and view our catalog of new and exciting
Children's Books